Adult Night

A T

Skate World

Christina Kallery

DZANC BOOKS

DZANC
BOOKS

www.dzancbooks.org

Adult Night at Skate World

Copyright © 2019 Christina Kallery

Originally published in print by dancing girl press & studio

The author wishes to thank the editors of the publications where some of these stories first appeared: Antithesis, Boxcar Poetry Review, The Collagist, Digging Through the Fat, Failbetter, Gargoyle, Golden Walkman Magazine, Marathon Literary Review, Mudlark, Rattle, and Stirring/ Sundress Publications, as well as Dzanc Books Best of the Web 2008.

Published 2021 by Dzanc Books

ISBN-13: 978-1-950539-62-8

Cover and title page designed by Emily Blair

Interior designed by XML Tricks

In memory of my mother,

Carol Elizabeth

CONTENTS

SWAN FALLS IN LOVE WITH SWAN-SHAPED BOAT

BERLIN (Reuters) - A swan has fallen in love with a plastic swan-shaped paddleboat on a pond in the German town of Muenster and has spent the past three weeks flirting with the vessel five times its size, a sailing instructor said Friday.

☆

He's not half nuts, this German swan, to love
something so near the actual, you might squint
from shore, squishing sand beneath your toes,
to see its broad white belly part the shining

green, neck angled always toward the clouds
deflecting every antic of its frenzied,
mini-suitor. This happens, right? Who among
us with a single red corpuscle hasn't dug in

and waited the whole doomed thing to its conclusion,
wanting some chill beauty to paddle its slow turn
toward us on the man-made lake? In your case,
not a Muenster tourist boat, let's hope, but more like

the narcissist with lovely eyes and a voice
to unzip things to, or the one that cut the right
profile but sank like a Petoskey stone. But still,
in spite of tearstains, sucker punches, fists to the glass

1

jaw, the dumb heart beats, then tries again. See,
there he goes, beak agog and hissing at the rival
birds, wings spread to seem more menacing, black
webbed feet paddling frantic through the algae.

Then night sets and a silver moon beams down
on bird and boat, afloat alone, and in the pale
light looking for all the world like the shape of love.

MISSED CONNECTIONS

"I look on here daily hoping someone noticed me enough to post an ad about it."

— *Anonymous in Trenton, Michigan*

✦

To the garbage man in the orange truck
who chatted up a lady by the Hollywood Tan,
would you guess she'd love another chance
to watch you hoist those overflowing cans?

And bashful guy from the drugstore line,
eyeing the pharmacist so cute it stirred in you
the first bright thrum of happiness in months.
How you waited to meet her gaze
as she counted your antidepressants,
pill by pill, into their amber jar.

And you, Billy the cable tech, with a gentle
side and cool blue eyes. You'd even fixed
that girl's computer desk, which you didn't
have to do.

O, single mom who bought a snake
at the Reptile Emporium. You so mesmerized
the assistant manager, the extra mice came free.

To Deb from the dollar store in Pontiac. Would it shock
someone among that throng who purchase sad-
eyed ceramic dogs to read that not a lone day fades
when you don't dream his face?

O, 38-year-old male from Waterford who likened
your love to a dumpster on fire. The odds
of the one you crave discovering this
amount to nearly zero.
Yet even you are no less lucky than all
us dingbat romantics the world over.
Our hearts electric with longing to touch
the impossible, the way lightning rips
its jagged course across the sky.

ADULT NIGHT AT SKATE WORLD

You'd think it was an eighth grade dance,
the way we stand shyly eying each other
when the first slow notes sound for couples' skate.

A fifty-ish man in a striped headband
and custom skates fit with blinking lights
asks *would I mind?* So we roll from the worn

carpet onto the glossy floor. One hand on my waist,
he gazes at a far wall and sings in high, quivering
tones to Endless Love. We pass a dozen

other couples: office managers in sport shirts,
single mothers squeezed into new jeans
and a few lone ones gliding through the tide of clasped hands.

Take the handsome man with dark hair swept
like a raven's wings from its stern middle part,
the moustache trimmed to a neat em-dash.

He moves like a figure skater, one long leg aloft
behind his jump-suited frame. No woman here tonight
can match his prowess as he weaves easy figure eights,

turns and sails backwards without a glance;
though I imagine his likely office job, manning
some cubicle in a gray and taupe-y sea

and the gaping dark that crouches nightly at his door.
Now the rink's Robert Plant commands the floor
beneath a silver disco orb and twirls once, twice,

a third time, pretending not to watch us
watching him. In his prime in '85, that bleached
mass of frizzed-out curls would have bobbed radiant

under hot stage lights during the guitar solo,
his attention rapt to the art at hand, yet aware
as a preening animal of the lip-glossed girls

in the front row whose eyes simmered
with envy and desire. But the gigs
have fizzled into soundlessness,

the Dodge van scrapped, the red guitar lies
long untuned in its velvet chamber.
Yet each Sunday at eight he pulls the black skates

from their nook and somehow finds a rhythm
not unlike rock and roll in this dim-lit dome
with its carnival colors and claw machine and women

fluffing their hair in restroom mirrors.
Just overhead hover the sour divorces,
languished careers, botched plans, those hours when life

took a sharp turn toward the inscrutable
and left us older and daunted in its wake.
But when the DJ calls the night's last song, we—

the lonesome and afraid, the jaded
and lost—peer through strobe lights
for somebody, if not lovable, then not a lunatic

and sing to a tune we first heard the summer
someone else left and we wept against a cool steering wheel
and felt the world spin, fierce and marvelous beneath our feet.

OUTSIDE THE LELAND HOTEL

One of my life's memorable kisses did not take place
sprawled on summer grass beneath Orion's belt
or on a chaste suburban doorstep after midnight,
only the hot and bothered crickets not asleep.
It was not a chaser to twenty-dollar cocktails in Manhattan,
nor the culmination of a long goodbye
before a yellow cab sailed into fog—

but after we left the almost empty theater with sticky floors
and emerged to find Detroit grown soft with falling snow.
After he'd steadied my elbow in the slippery lot
and cleared the windshield of the car I'd driven,
one wiper not right, down I-75 to pick him up.

And after we parked in the yellow glow
of his apartment building, fat snowflakes descending
on a homeless guy who waited outside
the passenger door to bum some change.
It was then he turned to me, tentative and gentle,
like a few faint notes plucked from a distant song.
And when we pulled away, his face
bore a softness that wouldn't survive
the cold walk from car to lobby.

I'm not writing about a man who loved me
With Byronic desperation
or a kiss that was sweeter than the rest.
And it's true that in an hour or two

the city's shimmering down would transfigure
into cardboard sludge and I'd be no closer to home.

I'm writing because I still recall this moment,
so bracing in its innocence, as heaven
seemed to fall, so slowly, around us.

ON THE LIST

Tonight, my friend is sad because
we couldn't get into The Magic Stick
to see some band. She wasn't on the list.
But I'm not thinking, "Get a real problem."
Nor will I remind her of the dying and the destitute.
I feel it like a grade school snub.

O List, I, too, have longed to be on you.
And for a few hours immune to life's
disparate assaults against my mattering
at all: form rejection letters, texts
that never return, backless medical gowns,
the clerk who eyes me like I'm fixing to filch some pens.

Inside the music thumps a smug refrain
as the bouncer's hairy forearm waves
on the cool, the black leathered,
the crusty guy who knew the MC5.
Our names are nowhere
for a girl with charcoal eyes to cross
off, so we could enter, feeling a little chosen.
We wouldn't even need a balcony seat or to make
out with the bassist on a disgusting couch.
We'd be content to stand before the stage
with our little plastic cups, belonging.

There's the list of the seventh grade lunchroom
to the nerd with his trembling tray;
or, to my aggrieved aunt, the clique lording

the list over the front pew of her Pentecostal church.
On the office list, the chisel-jawed glide
like yachts on an indigo sea, past frumpy rowboats
to their island of promotions.

As twilight drapes its purple cape across the sky,
we stand, dust off our skirts and settle for the neon
of an all-night diner in Hamtramck.

The way all our lists resolve in time,
to an ever-smaller, brighter orbit;
where plus one means there's someone to watch a movie with,
a flick that's not that great but has its moments.
Someone to call when the dark fog of aloneness looms,
Or to sit with on the front porch and watch the lunar eclipse—
its halo scripted on the broad black night
that goes on without us forever.

DRUNK GUY POEMS

✦✦

poetry readings have to be some of the saddest
damned things ever,
the gathering of the clansmen and clanladies,
week after week, month after month, year
after year,
getting old together,
reading on to tiny gatherings,
still hoping their genius will be discovered.

— Charles Bukowski

Drunk guy poems have to be some of the saddest
damned poems ever. The drunk guy pounding
on his typewriter, night after night, drink
after drink, smoke after smoke, getting old
alone, still believing like an angst-eyed
teen in the genius of self-annihilation. Grizzled
codger in his dingy underpants, hurling *fuck*
yous from a shadeless windowpane or strung
out and spitting in the yellow eye of dawn,
smirking as the suits trail off to work.

Or the poems where the drunk guy screws
a prostitute, then opines on love's brutality
while she's splayed, half-hammered
on his sweaty mattress (naked chicks swap
places in these drunk guy poems
like a porno Changing of the Guard).

Or maybe it's a close-up of a homeless
wino's mottled face, a barmaid's sagging
breasts, a batty crone squawking toothless
curses at imaginary foes. Take a moonlight
skinny dip in life's rank undertow,
bear witness to the crusty braggadocio,
the swagger of self loathing, an artsy
middle finger, an I told you so
deducing once for all that life is sad
and failure certain as a last call tab.
And it's braver, stronger to withhold
compassion from the world than give
and end up someone's chump.

He may as well be some lost hero from a comic book --
whiskey-breathed, box-jawed and jaded
a single jagged, scar etched on his cheek,
tapping out another tome at 3 am while neon
flickers live nude girls or xxx across his bedroom wall,
far off a lonely sax moans in the gloom: a scene
as far from real as superman or cowboy shows.

So flick on the dull fluorescent lights down at the Y,
cue up the cappuccino maker at the coffee shop,
turn down the football playoff at the open mic.

Give me the tax preparer whose bald patch goes pink
when he recites his sonnets of a long-gone lover's thighs,
the aging rocker's riff on Kerouac, the lady with a bad

dye job on being 18, knocked up and slinging pancakes
at a Big Boy, the gangly kid whose voice breaks
like a brittle reed when he talks about his dad,
the gray-haired man in a faded beret
whose refrain is always revolution.

Give me the quivering lumps of midlife
flesh, the young with incandescent, thrumming hearts
the old ones scorned by life and loathe to leave,
the weird and outcast, the perilously shy,
the crackpots, the rat raced, the subdivision dreamers.
Everyone tremulous for a little love and the sound
of a few hands clapping.

SQUATTER

I did not invite you, you pay no rent.
Formal demands go yet unmet.
Envelopes stack beneath the door.

How the heck did you get in? A forgiving
lock, a curtain shirring in the hopeful
spring, the back door ajar a moment too long?

I wish you'd at least fix up the place. The walls
need paint, dried insects dot
the dusty ceiling lamp, the fridge holds just two
takeout cartons and a jar of fancy mustard.
The couch springs sag your outline.

And when someone nice comes to inquire
they see your light in an upper room,
silhouette shadowing the cold pane
your smoke rings curling out the window,
widening, o by o, into the night.

HARVEST MOON ON TRASH NIGHT

Hauling out the last black Hefty bag
I spot the full moon fat as a lemon bundt
cake above the dumpsters. Three stray cats
dart into spindly elms that split the reeking

bins from the railroad tracks beyond. At night,
steel freighters thunder through here, jittering
loose windows, sounding their low drone
that strikes the heart's anvil like longing.

This is the sort of place you live when you don't
know where to go — young couples dreaming
lifetimes in their first shared beds, guys
who know too much about kung fu films,

or the just-divorced getting by between
visitation Sundays. I've grown to hate this
sameness, the nowhere feel of modest brick,
communal lawn plots, strip malls of the soul.

But tonight the big moon stops me cold; haloing
the slate October sky and wisped by clouds,
like the sky one autumn years ago.
After a nightmare kept me up, my mother laced

her boots and walked with me around our northern
town to help me sleep. Down past dark
houses to the street of empty shops that faced
the shore. Far below, I knew, black waves

of Lake Superior rushed the rocky crags.
In the quiet night that already smelled of snow
we heard the constant, churning undertow.
The moon looked near enough to touch

the unleafed limbs or if I stretched my palm,
I might feel its scarred and dusty face,
so many miles from home.

AT THE DOLLAR STORE

✯

Artificial lemon and plastic
clot the air, while fluorescent lighting
glowers down like an alien sun
upon the shelves of imitation china,
bins of flip-flops and American
flag bandannas. At the counter, a teenage
clerk with a silver cell phone at his ear trains
one eye on me, watchful, I suppose,
of the Lover brand condoms, men's
rhinestone rings, laser key chains.
In the center aisles beneath security
mirrors stand rows of ceramic bric-a-brac:
tearful clowns clutching balloon
bouquets, the Virgin Mary in her blue,
glitter-flecked robe, her pale, raised
palm more "take me to your leader"
than "behold, the Blessed Mother."

A boy whines to his mother for an orange water gun
one aisle down where toys look almost aware
of their cheap manufacture: the imitation
Barbie dolls with wiry hair who'd swab the Dream House
toilets, paunchy, imposter Godzillas alarming
to no one and nameless super heroes
in tacky capes and masks — their powers
long forgotten or inspiring no faith.

Then toward a back corner where pot scrubbers
like bright sea creatures commingle
with ineffectual garden tools.
Here, the crunch and press of harried lives bear down
in a flurry of ordinariness: day-glow
dish soap and off-brand sloppy joe mix,
hair pins and baby bottles, small needed things
that recall my mother collecting dusty change
from the bottom of a dressing table drawer
to buy something I had asked her for
—ice cream or a candy bar—
and often there was just enough, amazing
in those days of so little and so much.

GOVERNMENT CHEESE

With the iron ore mine laying off almost
everyone in town, we all got the government

cheese. It came in a cardboard box each month,
rectangle of orange American, so heavy

it could be a weapon—one blunt blow to an intruder's
skull and he'd never be the same. Good thing

there weren't many intruders to worry about.
My stepdad was a welder when the union

sent them home, saying things might turn
around, there might be another job. There

wasn't. For that nervous year, nobody ate
at restaurants, the neighbor's wife split town, we wore out

the knees of our jeans. Did they make the cheese
in factories like steel mills, where molten liquid

was forged into steel beams? Cooling golden
slabs sailing along assembly lines on their way

to become something else: pickup trucks or grilled
between slices of cottony bread. The government

cheese was good—creamy, melt-in-your-mouth, rich
taste, like things they say in those commercials.

WEST ELM CATALOG

Whoever might perch on this velveteen
couch never ate pizza
off a grease-soaked paper plate, alone
in their underwear at 1 am.
Look at the fringed throw tossed
just-so over one arm, how a single cup skims
the coffee table's smudge-less sea.

In the Urban Collection bookshelf,
several uncracked guides to Danish
architecture and a stack of foreign journals
keep their canny distance from framed
photographs in black and white.
No self-help tomes urge anyone
to Lose Weight Fast, Find Happiness
in 30 Days or claim It's Not Too Late
for Love. And not the smug restraint
of those two shelves, empty save
for a few ceramics and a thick-skinned plant.

There's no wrong note to cull
from that vintage record rack, curated
gravely as the Guggenheim. The balance
of iconic rock to soul to classic jazz,
seasoned by a few obscurities,
may have been calibrated by a physicist.
The same guy, perhaps, who stocked
the pantry with its photogenic jars.

And in the bedroom, the sheets' light shirring
hints: someone elegant has lounged here.
The pillowcases free of snot and tear stains
where no one grieves or fucks or dreams too long.
And in the corner where the tempered
morning gleams, a well-appointed desk.
A few strewn pencils sketch a dream
that's polished, clean and neatly traced,
the perfect showing of a life lived tastefully
not at all.

PRIZE PIG

A big pink pig—Grand Champ, no less—dozes
in the sunny dirt, domed belly swelling tidally just past
the screw-tailed rump. It looks a little like a naked fat man

snoozing at the fair—refugee from a California
nudist camp or party gone all wrong. Bristled back,
pink shoulders sloping vulnerable, while one ear flicks

a fly. A boy with cornsilk hair works up the guts to stretch
a skinny arm between the bars and poke its flank.
That's all we want sometimes—to touch the alien

and ugly things, and know them beautiful.
A plaque above the hog pen reads Purchased
by Kowalski so by Christmas he'll be sausages,

breakfast links and hams. But today is not a day to die—
soft earth, late August sun, the smell of deep fried
Twinkies carried on the breeze. A human palm warm

on tired flesh pats gently, tentative with awe
and the boy's small face delighted like he's seeing
not an exhausted pig, but fireworks, a big top show,

the bright world from a Ferris wheel 200 feet below.

THE ELVIS

I bet he gets some action, my friend says
of the guy onstage in pompadour and sky
blue pants, belly flanked by a doublewide
belt. It's Saturday night in a Polish bar outside

Detroit where everyone's already good
and drunk by the time he launches into Love
Me Tender, hauling out his stash of drugstore
scarves to drape, like gauzy blessings,

on the napes of women in the crowd,
a gesture that could pass for almost-love
in any other setting. There's something
of the real King's fervid charm that douses

lonely patrons clutching dollar beers—
how he'd inhabit any place you put him,
and even on some antiseptic '50s set,
his eyes would flicker into smile mid-

song and you knew he'd seen a pretty girl.
We watch our Elvis gyrate on the dingy stage,
beaded fringe aflail like there's no moment
more glorious than this one: Suspicious Minds

cued up on crackling speakers, sweaty bodies
swaying on the floor, another round to go
before someone hits a light switch and it's out
into the frozen streets, the way we all recall

the words to *wise men say, only fools rush in*
and it rises like a hymn into the rafters.

BOOGIE FEVER: A SESTINA

No illusions in its neon sign—a Tom Jones platform boot—
no frosted glass to fancy up the place. Just bald desire
ogling from the bar or backlit disco floor.
Life's too short for shame at Boogie Fever,
where spike-haired guys with biceps bulging
from their shiny shirts cruise like Mylar sharks in rainbow lights,

where receptionists eye college boys in baseball caps, light
menthol cigarettes, swap yarns of giving faithless men the boot.
It's any night in 30 years of singles bars—limp pick-up lines, the bulge
of mid-life run amok. Manmade fabrics scintillate desire
like heat lightning from the swell of breasts and pecs; call it fever,
that rank and primal longing lunging awkward on the floor,

the bass line thumping all the way to coat check. Up a floor,
we watch them dancing in their squares of light—
the bachelorettes with naughty hats, the claims adjusters, fevered
and forlorn, inching toward two girls in go-go boots
who slightly shift aside, deflecting all that sad desiring
borne of infinitesimal failures. The crowd heaves and bulges

like a lung to AC/DC, Donna Summer, bulging-
ruffled 80s Prince. Then a circle widens on the floor
around a mall-cop who can breakdance, his back-spins like desire
for spiral arms in a sky bereft of starry light;
he's followed by a guy in bolo tie and cowboy boots
who jerks and struts a vision of what boogie fever'd

look like as a real affliction — lurching, pop-eyed, feverish,
limbs aflail and rump out of control. Oh bulge
of lycra'd sassiness! Oh synthesizer'd beat! But he gets booted
by some chick in shocking pink who works it while the floor
bulbs flicker crazily below and spotlights
shine on strangers drunk and sloppy with desire.

Tonight I've learned a thing about desire —
your palm against the hollow of my back imprints its fever
as the crowd is belting out "The Gambler," and disco lights
cavort like fireflies while my dumb heart bulges
in its bony cage. We're swaying like first lovers on the floor;
next week you're heading back to Butte

but this minute what I most desire is here, amidst the bulging
mass of lonely souls on Boogie Fever's multicolored floor.
What unexpected happiness, these lights beneath your boots.

I HAVE ISSUES

The woman's t-shirt says in big
block letters stamped across her breast,
a self-help scarlet A. I spot her by the Polish
sausage cart clutching a corndog on a stick.

It's not so much the grand admission
of screwedupness to this crowd: bored carnies,
a boy with pale eyes so sad it's startling,
the lovers with their palms stuffed down

each other's back jean pockets. It's more the way
her face looks tranquil, as if the pressure's off.
Like in Sunday altar calls I witnessed as a kid
where some mammoth, grizzled guy might

heed the preacher's call to come down front
for prayer and end up slumped into the scratchy carpet,
a lump of snot and bellowing too hard for words
while the congregants all bowed their heads.
Don't let that be me, I'd pray as if this urge to bare

it all were catchy like a whooping cough or bad pop song,
a contagious, losing hand in strip poker of the heart.
And afterward, he'd struggle upright, flushed
pink-eared and bleary-eyed, to hoist his bulk into a cool

wood pew, and for a moment when he stood above
us all I'd glimpse a soft and yielding look
where all that pain had been, the whole human wreck
of what the shrinks call issues, battered and beloved.

THE NEST

⭐

The day after the rainstorm I find the nest —
crosshatch of wet grass and feathers
near the flank of rusted drainpipe in the yard.

A fat sparrow darts from the wreckage
into a sagging elm, and I spot among the twigs
and fluff an unfurled claw, slit of bulbous eye

and a delicate beak unveed to the morning sun.
Unsettling the whorls I remember
how after the worst of our fights at the end,

you were once compelled to bury a dead
bird like this one, nondescriptly black or brown,
found in an Amoco parking lot.

And when you told me I flinched
in disgust at the garish flailing
of your heart, how you relished your suffering

without me. Now I collect the damp assemblage,
careful not to drop the small body still entwined
there and imagine you on that sleeting December

day, in your too-thin blue jacket as you stopped
to consider the stiff-legged young grackle at the foot
of a pump, the way you folded the remains

into a days-old newspaper, seeing the first fronds
of adult feathers with their rainbowed sheen
among the fledgling down, the beads of eyes half-shut,

the beak agape and the little curled claws.
This morning I hold my own small dead weight,
hide it in the cool dark soil beneath the chrysanthemums

and in this still moment, I believe your outsized gesture
within the lesser one, mourning a loss that fits
in your palm when large ones fall with resolute

thunder from the sky.

UNDERPANT RAGE BURNS DOWN HOUSE

✦

*— An angry husband who threw old clothes
from his wardrobe in the garden
and set fire to them because he
could not find his clean underpants
accidentally burnt his home down.*

You know that in his nightmares it came
differently, the final great disaster that would set
his life ablaze. On his Posturepedic matress,
the angry husband maybe dreamt of F5

twisters, black as smoke and roaring from
the skies, or swollen tidal waves deleting
Albuquerque in one apocalyptic sweep. Perhaps
he figured doom would fashion him heroic—

the pistol-toting burglars tackled as a single shot
is fired, so wife and sons and Labrador can flee
while he slumps, alone and bleeding as the world
recedes to a single brilliant pinpoint of eternity.

But instead of cataclysmic bursts, he lives
with ordinary griefs and small domestic wrongs:
light bulbs dead in moth-strewn ceiling lamps,
the countless eye-rolls at his jokes, engine oil

grown sticky as La Brea tar. He'd maybe born it all
with grace so many years that overlooking stuff
became a kind of art. And in his mute, forsaken heart,
this guy was pissed that life had issued him

a plastic tray to the buffet line while others got to feast
in banquet halls. He'd had it on that dismal morning,
when, fresh-showered in his navy robe that someone
gave him Christmases ago, he found the top drawer bare

save for a wrinkled handkerchief and lone, black sock.
And if the wrong thing went missing at the crucial moment,
maybe even you would sprint just like a nutcase to the yard,
half-dressed and screaming curses so the neighbors

wonder did you find your wife in bed with some buddy
from the pub? Was it her lover's underpants you hurled
earthward the way a tortured opera star might fling his cape?
Is that why you crouch with your Bic lighter, almost gleeful

as an orange glow blooms amid the lump of underthings,
then spreads to beanstalks, peas and marigolds, engulfing everythi
that's green until your face drowns in the flickering,
too late in comprehending you create your hell.

TRYING TO START THE VAN

This cement-skied morning in Hell's
Kitchen—which sounds like we'd be roasting
on our feet—ice rings tailpipes in the street
as the engine of a dingy van strains,
chokes and sputters like a felled
wildebeest or drunk with whooping cough.
It's an old white Ford with scraped-off
lettering, that once was maybe driven
by a carpet guy or extermination crew.
A van churned out by workers in a factory
in Detroit, the kind I used to pass on 94
back home, snaking between smokestacks,
everything the color of rust.

The van's still wheezing in the gutter
while a black town car gleams by.
So I watch and wish the thing
would start, not only for the driver,
now awfully late to somewhere,
but the once-sleek engine now agasp
in dead cold. For the guys from that factory,
long laid off and dozing in front of talk shows,
braving another round of want ads,
or taking drive-thru orders and whatever work
that comes. And for Detroit, its heart of steel
and rubble, the unglamorous, needful grit that set
the world in motion and gave us songs to sing.
I'm rooting for them all, for that gray
belch and rumble to finally take this time,
as the starter fires and turns over,
over and over again.

WATCHING THE BEARS: BIG BAY, MICHIGAN

☆

For years before cable TV hit, the Big Bay dump
was semi-famous in nearby towns. On warm
nights, cars came crunching up the gravel road

headlights dimmed, the way you'd sneak into
the drive-in when the movie'd started. Except
there was no Spielberg blockbuster, no enormous

kisses, magnificent explosions, not even a pale
screen to loom over acres of spiky evergreens. Instead,
entertainment was the live, black bears that ate

the garbage at the dump. Families in station wagons,
college kids crammed into someone's rusted El
Camino, windows rolled low and daring as the bears

appeared from the edges of darkened woods and lumbered
out to feast on Quarter Pounder crusts, table scraps
and mozzarella glued to pizza boxes. Black furred

haunches glistening, they pawed through bags
with happy snorts and grunts, easy meals to come by
after months of snowy sleep. One eve, a young guy brave

with a few too many beers got close enough to lob
his empty bottle at a bear as the big head turned,
round ears cocked flat, and lunged, while the drunk kid

sprinted on watery legs and dove into the waiting car,
his buddies slamming the door in time to dodge
an angry swipe that left a furrow in the driver's side,

souvenir for overstating his rank in the world.
Who knows if they considered their pal's brush
with being lunchmeat or just headed off to town, tossing

back more bottles, blasting Zeppelin's Black Dog, stopping to chat
up a chubby barmaid at the Crossroads Tavern on 480, the last
letters in its red sign flickering, the only light for miles.

BURNOUTS

Downriver Detroit, 1987

"There's enough burnouts out there to go hands across America"
>   *— Heavy Metal Parking Lot*

"I went to a party last Saturday night. I didn't get laid, I got in a fight."
>   *— Lita Ford*

You'd see them rolling joints in class, textbook propped
to hide the task, feathered hair fringing their eyes,
a starter mustache shadowing their upper lips. Always
a few hanging out on empty bleachers, trading swigs
from something bottom shelf in a paper bag.

And always the jagged lettered logos of their concert tees,
their suede boots like the ones worn by the guy in 7th hour
fine arts. He pulled them on every day, in snowbound
December and blazing June, laced to the knee over jeans tight
as snake's skin, belt buckle shaped like a woman's
clutching hand forever poised just short of third base,
a heavy metal send-up of the poet's Grecian urn.

I never knew his name, but I recall his cloud-grey,
half-mast eyes, his Bic-penned scrawls
of fiery skulls and undead guitarists,
his public makeouts with some girl by the acrylic paints.
He'd float through hallways, an apathetic ghost
gliding onward to its dead-end job, jail term

or other bad turn. But it would be sweet
justice if he dodged the old clichés and got by ok.

It would be a flipped bird from the window of a black
Camaro they said would never make it off the blocks—
watch it peel onto the entrance ramp, rebuilt engine roaring,
to catch the last gleam of sunlight fading fast behind the
trees.

Acknowledgements

Antithesis	"West Elm Catalog"
Boxcar Poetry Review	"Boogie Fever: A Sestina"
	"The Nest"
The Collagist	"Trying to Start the Van"
	"Watching the Bears: Big Bay, Michigan"
Digging Through the Fat	"Burnouts"
Failbetter	"Swan Falls in Love with Swan-Shaped Boat"
Gargoyle	"Government Cheese"
Golden Walkman Magazine	"Outside the Leland Hotel"
Marathon Literary Review	"Missed Connections"
Mudlark	"Prize Pig"
	"The Elvis"
Rattle	"Adult Night at Skate World"
Stirring/Sundress Publications	"Drunk Guy Poems"
	"Harvest Moon on Trash Night"
	"Underpant Rage Burns Down House"

"Swan Falls in Love with Swan-Shaped Boat" was nominated for a Pushcart Prize and reprinted in Best of the Web 2008, by Dzanc Books.